Cynthia Antoinette Roomes

EVOLUTION

A Collection of Paintings Poetry and Prose

AuthorHouse™ UK Ltd.
1663 Liberty Drive
Bloomington, IN 47403 USA
www.authorhouse.co.uk
Phone: 0800.197.4150

Published by AuthorHouse 06/18/2013

ISBN: 978-1-4772-3792-2 (sc)
978-1-4772-3793-9 (e)

Any people depicted in stock imagery provided by Thinkstock are models,
and such images are being used for illustrative purposes only.
Certain stock imagery © Thinkstock.

This book is printed on acid-free paper.

Dedicated to the readers, the viewers,
the listeners and the doers - the lovers of the arts.

List of Contents I

List of Contents II

NOTE: *original artwork produced as gouache on paper*

Cynthia Antoinette Roomes

Evolution

A Collection of Paintings Poetry and Prose

About the Author and the Book

Born to Jamaican parents on the 6th day of December 1959, I painted the 'Evolution' exhibition of artwork over a period of 22 years starting at age 30, the poetry and prose evolved over more time than that, about 40 years in all. Now I am in my 53rd year it is time to share my first amalgamated collection with a public audience.

I want to take the reader and the viewer on a journey through my evolution as a black woman, exploring what it means to live in a disadvantaged urban area, to be uplifted and inspired by the therapeutic and explorative qualities of visual art, and the written and spoken word.

The Original Inspiration

'Evolution' provides an insight to my thoughts and feelings as an adolescent and young adult growing through to maturity in the often turbulent inner city area of Brixton in Lambeth – an eclectic and diverse south London borough, known as much for the urban riots of the 80s, as for its market place, artist community, entertainment venues, the Brixton Village Food Hall and other eateries, and its vibrant nightlife.

I am one of many black people born into a community of commonwealth migrants from the Caribbean, made to feel less than welcome, left wondering why our parents were invited here in the first place, and what to do about the dilemma - after I discovered it, in order to progress and succeed in British society.

Impact of the World View

The world has changed rapidly, the cold war, proliferation of nuclear weapons, mass demonstrations and protests, racial tensions and the international space programme were all headline news when I was growing up. I remember being particularly traumatized by images of famine in Biafra and Ethiopia, by the wars in Vietnam, Israel and Northern Ireland. I was challenged by the impact of communism in the Caribbean, Poland, USSR and China, angered by apartheid, and disappointed by the role of the West in the whole sorry mess.

Therapeutic Values

Like many people, I was consequently alienated and angst ridden. I sought a spiritual solution to material problems over which I had no control, and yet many years later I am no more assured by the current economic crisis, the state of the middle-east, the endless stream of wars, and the issue of environmental sustainability.

By exploring myself and my evolution through the medium of art poetry and prose, I found a way for negative energy to be converted into something positive. There is therapy in art and literature, an infinity of space in which both the artist, the reader, the listener and the viewer can share similar and disparate experiences in a 'safe' place.

The 'Evolution' Collection

The 'Evolution' collection is illustrated by a selection of my poetry, and by three segments of prose designed to add to the reader and viewer experience by permeating what is seen with what is spoken. I invite you to join me on an interactive journey through a lingering lattice work of carefully curated images and words, dug out from deep within my soul.

CAR: September 2012

Not All At Once ...

(advice for the reading of my poems)

1 - is good
2 - you could
3 - I would
but more
than 4
you should explore
with caution.

5 - is live
you will
survive
6 and 7
on route
to heaven
but do proceed
with caution.

Part One

BEGINNING

Thoughts On Nothing

'Nothing' can be understood as a recurring feature in a series of three part sequences in which something is and / or was (involved):

Sequence One:

'Nothing' is a precursor to time and space.

'Something' comes out of time and space.

'Nothing' is the end of time and space.

Sequence Two:

If we utilise time and space ineffectively we produce nothing, become nothing.

If we utilise time and space effectively we produce something, become something.

If we utilise nothing we run out of time and space and nothing results.

Sequence Three:

Nothing and something are inextricable parts of time and space.

Nothing often leads to something in time and space.

Something often leads to nothing in time and space.

Sequence Four:

Nothing is the '0' in 0 1 2;

Something is the '1' in 0 1 2;

Time and Space is the '2' in 0 1 2.

Sequence Five:

'Nothing' is the critical mass

From which 'something' is drawn

In 'time and space'.

Sequence Six:

Something	- more to be done	= objective of a continuum
Something	- needs to be done	= opportunity arises
Nothing	- more to do	= objective achieved
Nothing	- more can be done	= opportunity ends
Something	- no longer occurs	= something becomes nothing
Nothing	- no time and space	= opportunity does not exist.

Timing

Millennia of familiars
Centuries of old
Decades of accolades
Years filled with tears
Months without fronts
Weeks without freaks.

Take time to wonder
Grow fonder
Of what matters most
In a host
Of competing choices.

Days in a haze
Hours with powers
That seemed to be
Minutes without limits
Seconds bring bonds
Between you and me.

Take time to wonder
Grow fonder
Of what matters most
In a host
Of competing voices.

Elements 1 – energy

At First...

At first the sound of water
Cool and fresh
Washing away the turmoil
In my thirsty soul
Love of my life
Quench me

Then the sound of music
Warm and soothing
Answering the call
Of my roaming spirit
Love of my life
Calm me

Then the sound of words
Wise and true
Confirming the thoughts
In my questioning mind
Love of my life
Answer me

Then the sound of heart beat
Loving faith and power
I adore the expectation of
Your arms around my body
Love of my life
Embrace me.

Elements 2 – earth

Creation

Who ordered the cosmos above
And formed it with all of his Love
Who caused the Sun and Moon to be
Who planted the seed for the tree

... a voice came right
out of the darkness and whispered unto me
I ...

Who made the lightening to flash
Who made the thunder to roll
Who made the earth to quake and shake
Who made tornadoes to blow

 ... a voice came right
out of the darkness and whispered unto me
I ...

Who made the rainstorms to howl
And hailstones to fall all around
Who made the snow so icy cold
Who made volcanoes explode

 ... a voice came right
out of the darkness and whispered unto me
I ...

Who loves Earth with all of his heart
Made woman and man from the start
Who showed the way to truth and right
Who brightened the path with His light.

 ... a voice came right
out of the darkness and whispered unto me
I ...

Elements 3 – water

The Unseen

I could not see you
But I could feel
Electro magnetic
Magnetising.

I want to see you
So I can feel
Skin to skin - without
Compromising.

I discovered you
Seemingly waiting there
With real loving
Vibrations.

I would like to explore you
So I am waiting here
No gravity - just great
Expectations.

Elements 4 – air

Astral Travel

Oh for a journey
Far out forward
From the past
Presently
Standing fast
Where radio waves
Vibrate the verily soul

Oh for an insight
To the blackness
A hidden zone
Wherein is sadness
One stands alone
And like a magnet
Draws one to one goal

The supreme good
A coppiced wood
A busy stream
Of ambitious dreams
A tranquil scene
Confirms we have
Arrived…

Elements

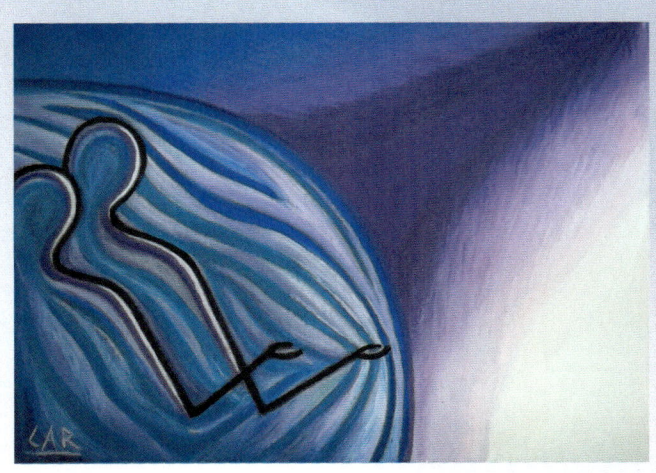

Part Two

DEPARTURES

Lost Eden

Is There 'Life' After 'Death'?

No - there is not 'life' after 'death'. In the sense of being conceived, being born, living, breathing, dying and death - when one is dead, one is dead.

However - there is scope for a 'continuum' which relates to electro magnetics, seismic and atomic energy, radio and sound waves, light and dark matter.

All these can be manipulated in the conscious and /or sub conscious mind of a living person to such an extent that they achieve or are afflicted with a 'continuum' after they are dead i.e. they manifest in an 'afterlife' only if death and 'nothing' is not to be their final destination - as yet. Pertaining to the 'manifestations' - some people can feel them, hear them and see them on the spectral planes of time and space.

The good who have progressed to a state of enlightenment during life are the 'achievers', the evil who have committed unspeakable sins during life are the 'afflicted'. The good trans-navigate to an 'afterlife' if they have a purpose to serve. The evil are transmigrated to an 'afterlife' if they have a sentence to serve.

They both reach an ultimatum, the time and space where they have satisfied the reason why they continue in the 'afterlife'. If the good can serve no further purpose, or when the evil have served their sentence, they both 'discontinue', they both become 'nothing'.

An equation controls the 'continuum', the balance between good and evil, during life and after death in the 'afterlife':
- the absolute harmony of the masculine and the feminine
- an explosive and dynamic equation in perpetuity
- high velocity fission and fusion
- the arcana of 'existence' itself.

In my humble opinion this is it, this is the answer to the question...

Reincarnated Souls

'At last', said I
'I have found the missing link'.
My wandering heart
a vast uncharted sea
is calmed and lulled
by a gentle breeze.
A whisper of hope
brings visions of how
to be free.

It was unimagined
by lesser mortals
a concept un-conceived
to be at peace within
the depths of another
in pure and high
mystical union
an eternity away
from The Original Sin

And I, in time
with heady euphoria
discard the gravity
releasing the weight
becoming light
I rise to my Love
who had waited a while
somewhat patiently
at an open gate.

And we, like old flames
burn fiery hot
in the heat of passion.
Cool in the aftermath
our celestial bodies
create systems in space
so the love of our hearts
can travel at will
a well trod path.

I recalled a previous time
when we embraced
dancing the steps of levity
seeking the field of permanence.
We were glad
for our second coming
finding that from before
we had sealed our conclusion
in the holiest alliance.

Ode to Eve

The magnetic attraction
Of forbidden fruit
A searing burning force
Insatiable desire
Resistance subdued
My opposing mind is mute
I crave to feel your consuming fire.

Such fire is quenched
Only by your water
Splashing and lapping
Against my inner walls
Calming me, gently loving me
Almost as a daughter
Created at your will
Inviting calls.

Quietly insistant rhythm
Swaying seductive move
But I am not to be seduced
I willingly receive your force
Penetrating slowly
We two, having nothing to prove
Enjoy forbidden fruit
From skin to source.

Am I to taste in fear
Of abstract punishment
Is not Heavenly fantasy
To become reality on earth
Will you fulfill your promise
Or were you sent
To taunt me. Still I drink
And savour the birth.

The knowledge of good and evil
To eat and know all
In my body and my mind
I cannot deny
The warmth I feel at your touch.
Let the fruit fall
Into my hand. Let us eat
To dare is not to die.

Much I Do Love You

How much I do love you?
With purpose I go on a journey
to discover the measure
of feelings pure and true.

I count all the starts in space
and view the expanse of sky
I weigh the mass of earth
and the tear that falls from your eye.

When all things are added together
and the totals are made right
there is no need for subtraction
just movements from dark to light.

How much I do love you
I would fail to ever contain
my desire to have you with me
in happiness and joy, bitterness and pain.

You stretched your hands to infinity
and wiped the tears I cried
what time there was you gave to me
there is justice because you tried.

Never my dearest darling one
will I leave your aching side
each wound I'll mend with wattle and daub
until time once more turns the tide.

Mother Earth

Part Three

Day

Primordial Soup – central

Dis-Located Arrival

We have arrived

at the dis-located area

joined.

Locate the joints

analyse

criticise

exorcise.

Also

Internally.

Dis-located

we are not to be.

A part of our preparation

is to be

apart from our separation.

Locate and integrate

retentions.

Locate and liberate

intentions

Non Renunion

I, being totally betrayed once
erect a sub-conscience defence
against re-occurrence.

I, being totally dependent
upon living love
sever all ties
existing on dreams
engendered by one
I thought
worthy of my attention
and devotion.
I was proven wrong
I was cheated and deceived
I had put upon a pedestal
an imperfection
ill conceived.

Upon his return
I reminisced
I recalled
memories
whose companion
was bitter pain.

I think not then
that this time
love lives once again.
In the incubator of life
I await another train.

Forget Me Not

Remember me with gladness
when I am gone
put away the sadness
knowing it won't be long
before I see you again
- at our beginning.

Do what I told you to do
when I was there
live according to what is true
without flinch or fear
in no mans land
- wars permitting.

Visit me whenever you can
from time to time
during a history that spans
the solemn climb
to our happiness
- tears allowing.

We never did talk about
how things would be
in the ensuing drought
separating you from me
time for a change
- in your living.

Forget me not and how it was
when we were together
fighting for the supreme cause
then – and now forever
let love rest in peace
- when you are remembering.

Part Four

NIGHT

Continents – broadband

Earth Struggle

Could not understand what the contention was for
at first I thought the two women were friends
that they were feeling alright within themselves
or so it did seem standing on the outside'
Still – I don't want to criticise
just bearing witness to my eyes.

Any how, there they was, standing in a square
full of granite stones with corners dark and gloomy.
Even in the dock, I can say I know I did see
a difference between them did arise
they started fussing and then a fight
even though it was day and not night.

I stood off to one side, glimpsed just one remaining
before the other one flew though loudly screaming.
She set a trap, then flung camouflage over
and went and hid to see what would happen.
I stand and observe
a ragged raw nerve.

As the manifest creation symbol
surely they could do much better. After all
they had family and children back home
but they set a stumbling block against each other.
Mother earth herself shook to rebel
one warring woman buckled and fell.

The foundations of granite stone started to crack
the other women dropped on her back
just missed the trap and looked afraid.
The other one grabbed a shovel and spade
then a concrete block smashed the ground
the woman in the dust spun around.

It just missed her head. Then again I saw the other one
Dust was flying – as yet no ashes
In the travelling of my mind I know there is a better way
to settle an argument, than to create destruction.
I covered my nose and my mouth
left them struggling in the south.

Tunnelling to Light

I am running through a concrete zone
conscious of an intention
to reach a goal.
Time being on my side
running was not a problem
I just chose to do so.
It was fitting
to the intention.

There was a tunnel and a flyover
it was a through and under
sort of thing.
Time being my eyes
I looked up and observed
unruly kind of children
playing away
on the flyover.

So as I was going under I eyes them
checking the actions of their hands
- they in particular
can halt times motion.
But they was just playing
in the way children do
wondering of course
at my intention.

I turned my eyes to the tunnel
glad for the circle of light
kind of inviting you know.
Time being my sensor
evidently this was the goal.
I was still running
having feared nought
of the flyover.

All things were in good order
time being my motion
checking the youth
under the flyover
through the tunnel
sighting the light
leading to the goal
with one intention.

History's Faded Negation

In my home town I recall well
the house of my history
even though it is no longer there
it formulated me.

I was there and conscious - more time
relaxing away back in the past
a cygnet was looking for his swan
found her at long last.

An interruption ensued - irritating
hovering at the open room door
I suspended my reasoning with the seeker
to find out what the stranger was looking for.

He had little to say that I could understand
so I stood at the portal impatiently
his image got permeated by air
he faded back in history.

I was living my story and he was a claimant
with no rights to my benefit
I was well - being into life and not stories
it was indeed I who held the writ.

Then I became glad at the sighting of memory
for this false claim to true history
was revealed for what it was
what he was - was not to do with me.

He was a was - and not an is to I
who being in the here and now
am happy he did show himself
at least now I know the how.

Tired of explanations and remonstrations
my will determined his non - existence
so there was now space outside the door
I could return inside and take up my stance.

Part Five

SETTLEMENTS

Totem

Social Anarchy

I Am Evolving

I am perpetually engaged in the fundamental aspects of organizational capacity, governance, fundraising and income generation – often in the government tent and campsite, sometimes lobbying or engaging on the outside too.

I increasingly see myself as an evolving 'social entrepreneur' (the community development kind) specialising in building and generating social capital, and seeking a social return on my investment, including the triple bottom line: environmental economical and social ethics.

The Anarchist

The 'anarchic' elements occur in the non-democracy of government, in the diminishing of people power, in the creation of unfair and disproportionate law, dictators, state oppression, or spending cuts that affect the most vulnerable whilst the culprits get away with their ill gotten gains.

So I quickly want to get out of the tent, away from the campsite, and to flee from any allusion that I am in collusion with an anarchic government or state system. But I have to consider a way to still do my job – generating and supporting the development of social capital. Because I am not the 'government', I become seen as the 'anarchist' if I challenge too hard, say too much, stowaway the party line in favour of the community line and the social endeavour.

Cohabitation

It would be a good outcome if the social entrepreneur - as defined by my own context, were to be seen as acceptable, to be heard and listened to, and for the powers that be to act upon 'information received'.

Better still if an 'anarchic government' begins to see itself and the social entrepreneur as having equal responsibilities in a pro-people state where constituents have not only a vote, but also real influence power and control which is welcomed in and around the tents on the campsite.

We should somehow be comfortable inhabiting the space side by side, or accept that being on opposite sides is part and parcel of democracy and that the government (anarchic or otherwise) should not then choose to stamp out opposition and rule with an iron fist, or with brutal military oppression using armed forces - as occurs all too frequently around the world and throughout human history.

Socially Acceptable Behaviour

There should be an acceptance that I have the right to be regarded as a citizen rather than an anarchist, and a celebration of the fact that I resist the inequality of the status quo, and insist on living up to humanitarian principles that may be out of sync with the policies strategies and practices of an anarchic government. This is the 'non-democracy', it suppresses, or does not do enough to support and create a platform for, the ethical business of evolving social entrepreneurs.

Look What You Doing

Look what you doing
What you think you doing to my people

Take the Red Indian man
Out of his own land
Then you put him on a reservation
Taking away his nation
Plundering his treasures
Take all the pleasure out of living

Look what you doing
What you think you doing to my people

Frustrate the Aborigine
Tell him he has no history
Then you populate his country with convicts
The owner you tried to evict
Pushed him in the outback
Exploit him until his back cracked

Look what you doing
What you think you doing to my people

Way over in New Zealand
Inhabited by the Maori Man
Became a sight for tourists to see
They checked how his culture pretty
Living like a tenant
A remnant of former glory

Look what you doing
What you think you doing to my people

And I an exiled African
See these things and over-stand
The west is devoid of feelings
I want no part of their dealings
They stole my inheritance
So yes – I was born with a grievance

Look what you doing
What you think you doing to my people

So what is the solution
I think it is a revolution
Tip the balance of power
This is their final hour
Make no excuses
They must pay for all their abuses

Look what you doing
What you think you doing to my people

Philosophical

I feel
and sometimes
I think
and so it is
therefore
I am.

I do
and sometimes
I do nothing
simply because
therefore
I can.

I want
and sometimes
I need
in the face of hunger
therefore
I scan.

The right
and sometimes
the wrong
a choice requiring
therefore
a plan.

The offence
and sometimes
the defence
often requires
therefore
sixth sense.

Fantasy
and sometimes
reality
are only the tip
therefore
of what we see.

Within yourself
and sometimes
beside yourself
knowing your purpose
therefore
is key.

Yearning   Feed

　　Desire   Perpetuate

　　　Passion   Sustain

　　　　Need   Life

Free   *We*

Spacious   *Us*

Dark   *Me*

　　Filling   Willing

Light   *You*

　　　　　　　　　FEELINGS

　Extending   Long

　　Filling   *Willing*

Light   *Warm*   *Strong*   We

　　Dark   Us

　　　Tender   *Loving*

　　Spacious   Me

　　　Free   *Feed*   You

　　Yearning   Desire

　　　Perpetuate

　Passion   Need

　Life   *Sustain*   Sustain

Perpetuate   Feed

Tender   *Life*   Loving

　Warm   Strong

　　Filling   *Need*   Willing

　　　Passion

　Extending   Long

　　Desire

　　Light   Dark

　Spacious   Free

You   *Yearning*   Me

Us   We

75

Love Life

To live <u>live</u> life
love like life
itself.

Live life like
life is love.

A love life
should be like
<u>live</u> life.

Love <u>live</u> life
live <u>live</u> love.

Living <u>live</u> love
makes me feel like
I am alive.

To live <u>live</u> life
live life like love
itself.

Part Six

ELEVATIONS

Twins

A State of Mind

Ipso facto
chaos confusion ignorance.
Playful youth
carefree
become dying shells
careworn.

Integral separation
threats of subjugation
wandering through a wilderness
searching for what
cannot be found.
And like fodder
foodstuff regurgitated
the substance is consumed
the waste is rejected
the core remains
used.

Prohibited and restricted
drained
of all but delusion
detained
in mysterious illusions.
An ordered dream
transport to awakened reality
a mind which knows
no difference
between death and sleep.

According to the measure
of this concrete time zone
nothing and nobody is real.
Unable to feel zeal

a stately mind elevates
and like a drone
quietly refuses
to be danger prone.

Ad infinitum
an abstract programme
makes compulsive choices
on anothers behalf
regardless of the voices
which said otherwise.
The comfort of knowledge
becomes a blessed release
to simply then
know the difference
between war and peace.

Phoenix Rising

Down below I surely know
there is no smoke without a fire
from whence the phoenix rises
to her great and blest desire.

So from fiery flames I do ascend
my aching heart hath no friend
I alone must care and tend
to fallen tears that hath no end.

Walking through a fallow field
the armour of God for my shield
where many sticks and jagged stones
would break my strong but weary bones.

I bear with love the heavy cross
of life without much light
I look upwards and ahead
to see a pathway shining bright.

Despite this world of morbid things
uplift the flight of open wings
stir the breeze that often brings
the song my soul so sweetly sings.

So I can rise and I can breathe
the faith that lives inside of me
a mind that knows of higher ground
shall not be claimed by misery.

Phoenix Rising

From Before

Previously, we had been friends
when rains fell and rivers ran
through hills and mountains
echoing sweet refrains.
Cascading fountains
frothing and foaming
gently corroding
sand and stones
there from creation.
The air was heavy with the scent
of lush vegetation.
Sun blest food, open shelter
a place to rest from play
which filled our day
with gladness.

maybe tomorrow we'll meet again
passing years move a little faster
and bring you to where I am.

Now we are separated souls
the rivers run dry
yet thunder rolls.
Valleys are haunted by the cries
of children taunted by the lies
which made them fatherless,
but still they are wanted.
Women singing lullabies
quietly caress skin and bones
starved from creation.
The air is rancid with the stench
of a dying population
and the sun takes no time to rest.
Their eyes are filled with tears
and bitter sadness.

maybe tomorrow we'll meet again
passing years move a little faster
and bring you to where I am.

War Bride

Our simple lives
my dearest soldier man
had simply become
part of the master plan.

You were conscripted and restricted
merely exercising the drill
learning the discipline
determining our will.

We had a parting
of body and soul
just as the half
divided from the whole.

Our happiness though measureless
was finite
indeed we would if only we could
reunite.

Defying the lying
of a vast machine
fast destroying
our childhood dream.

Still - within my heart
you lay to rest and remain
the start of an end to our beginning
leaving me to feel your pain.

I do not find glory
in the state emblem
crying 'Honour in Death in Victory'
grief - is my problem.

Living in hope in faith
in loving memory
I raise your vision borne in me
a seed fulfilling need.

I sought no hero carved in monuments
of wood and stone
whilst from a platform in a trench
condolences - in monotone.

Trinity

Part Seven

IMPROVEMENTS

Re-gained Garden

Mankind Know Thyself

Though it is true to say
mankind has evolved
and the current species
is somewhat distinct
from earlier versions
id est - the Neanderthal
is said to be extinct.

The power hungry madness
of an ignorant man
is difficult to extinguish
but easy to distinguish
from the egalitarian
hopes and ambitions
of a humble man.

And so it is...
the commune of humanity
cannot flourish
in the fullness of reality
for many it remains a dream
for others it is the subject
of social mobility.

A revolutionary aspiration
sought out and fought out
on urban battlefields
by any means necessary.
But in the aftermath
who is left to answer the question
about sustainability.

Better

If I could
hold your hand
and walk with you
through
this landscape
if we two
could then do
better
would you.
Then walk with me
so we can bebetter.

For the world
of human people
and animals
and rivers
and straight canals
leading to
a landscape
where things are
better.

If you and me
do walk that way
could we make a day
that is better.
Would me and you
become one
seeing to it that
evil was done
and finished
and long gone
so that the next day
would be better.

How can we know
which way to go
when the path is littered
with the blood
of the innocent
shed by the hands
of those who are
ignorant.

So we wallow through
and swallow
bitter pills
for our health
and the re-distribution
of wealth.
Heading for a goal
defended
by the righteous soul
in the hope
that things will be
better.

Exploding the Myth

See those wrinkled faces
in far off lands
where white flags are flown
and sad eyes cry
in fear of the unknown.
Forced to walk in columns
to follow and comply
in the absence of social deviancy
and the unanswered question 'Why?'

Do people choose their leaders
to make global crisis news
to reign in power oblivious
to subjugate their views.

Catch twenty-two
a faulty exit
once caught is one to remain
between parallels of left and right
in the centre of political gain.
And in the media malaise
parties join, coalesce and fool
with a catalogue of sound bite contingencies
from a PR market selling new PC cool.

Do people choose their leaders
to hear when they refuse
to live in poverty regardless
to merge their shades of red and blue.

In the arena all do walk
Utopias Road
in search of hopes and dreams
but my Utopia is not yours
and theirs is not what it seems.
Still the wrinkled faces
bring forth, raise and rear
smooth visages, with sparkling eyes
that will shed the same old tears.

Do people choose their leaders
to destroy with acid corrosion
to erect façades that promote a myth
to wait for a big bang explosion.

Part Eight

CONTINUATION

Self

I Am That I Am

Chapter One

As a child, to understand 'who am I' (a question I might ask of my 'self') and 'who I am' (an assertion about my 'self' that I might put to others), I ask many questions and pursue knowledge through learning. I go to church and I love God diligently. I develop a sense of my 'self' in that given context.

Chapter Two

As a young person moving through to adulthood I think about my name, where it came from and what it means. I learn from my parents and family about my culture and heritage, I engage in curriculum based learning, I read many books, I am creative, socialise, experience good and bad, learn right from wrong. I develop an awareness of evil, and I consciously choose to walk a path away from doing evil deeds. I evolve a response to the questions 'who am I and who I am' because I know my 'self'.

Chapter Three

Then little by little as the years go by – remembering my Creator as in the days of my youth (ref. KJV Ecclesiastes 12), I build on the foundations of 'who am I and who I am' by developing principles based on what I want to be, to have, to give, to receive – in life and work and love. Then I live according to those principles and by so doing - in the age of my maturity, 'who I am' is 'what I am', and conversely 'what I am' is 'who I am'. I am in control of my 'self'

Chapter Four

This manifests through 'what I do'. I become 'what I am and I am that I am'. My 'self' is subsumed by the 'I am' - a fluid organic dynamic evolution, past present and future. I am an ongoing process of developing, learning about, knowing and controlling my 'self'.

Reflections

I beheld myself
in front of the mirror
beholding suddenly
someone switched on the camera
and sent images
flashing across the screen.

And then captions
from the minds of others
trying to show me
thoughts
thinking
what the I AM means

And options
getting lights from a tube
getting plights from a woman
getting fights from a community
some distance away
deep and pensive
in the mirror
like an oasis.

Then the nomads came
to drink water from my well
at first
they could not handle the swell
and so their desire tilted
their minds wilted
as does growth of blossoming kinds
in a dry and arid desert.

The vision dissipated
I anticipated
my expectations
and suppressed their qualms
becoming calm
like sand and seas
without breeze
but with fire
bringing one coming
to ones knees
with desire.

Burning bright
dark ashes
black
and back
to the mirror.

I would be loved
as I am
had I succumbed
had I appeared
as desired appearances
I would have been seen
by others
as a stranger
on my own screen.

But I recognized my face
had been to that place
had filled empty space
had been left alone
visionary
but lonely.

When I said
'end the plight, do the right'
my teachers they did scold me.
When I said
'sight the fight, dark to light'
my family never told me …

About tired ancestors
swathed in sacraments
dripping with blood
their tears make mud
and rivers that flood
my family never told me …

About skin flesh and bone
carved in monuments
of wood and stone
who wail and moan
how could I leave myself
danger prone.

They deflected my ammunitions
from history and futuristically.
They deflected my ammunitions
gain said from magazine publications
- they almost convinced me.

But the ancestors said
'Is not your eye full of beauty?'
'aye' - replied I
and then saw beauty in I.
Eyes is - beautiful.

Mama Cry, Mama Cry

Mama cry mama cry
Mama cry living eye water from her eyes
mama cry so 'til she no have no more
eye water to cry, mama cry.

Things was really hard living on an island
then came a man in a shirt and tie
from the mainland.
Saying 'free education
in our modern civilisation
good working conditions for all
high wages unlikely to fall
all you got to do is give us your labour
get on a boat a plane a train
and come on over'

Mama leave mama leave
mama leave the little island in the sun
mama leave and say she soon send for the youth
and let them come, mama leave.

Yes labour was what they wanted
slaving on the mainland.
Rushing like a russian through the concrete
mama was missing the beach and the sand.
Feeling the cold of ice and snow
smelling the paraffin fire glow,
mama recall granma mention plantation
then she find herself in the same situation,
all she could do is send for the children
the few shilling she save must can educate them.

Mama send mama send
mama send for the youths to make them get wise
mama send for the youths she borrow she lend
from friend and friend, mama send.

But things was getting worse
when the youths reach the mainland,
the natives get worried and started to curse
people from the island.
It's true they did get some schooling
yet still the teachers was only fooling,
feeding the youth a history full of lies
with mind control they tried to hypnotise.
Some loose through they choose to play the game
some win through they know that all is the same.

Mama why mama why
mama why so suffer so much when you try
mama why should I give and live like a fool
when I know that you cry.

mama why - mama cry
mama try - mama sigh
then she say
'children never you believe a lie
always look your friends in the eye
and remember
try to remember
always remember
mama cry, mama cry'.

A Free Ka

Walking with determination
high on our creativity
alongside
The Time of Judgement.
Talking losses and gains
lightning flashes
with thunder
and seismic energy.
We walk in a train
reasoning.

The space
gained dimensions.
we progressed
to the greater
and did satta
loving.

Two whites entered
previously being there
doing their own thing
but watching.
We eyes them up
and look them down.
Music was playing
when we heard them say
'it's bigger in here
we could have hired this place
if only we did know'.
We hear them
we blank them
continuing where we start
heart to heart.

A party of explorers
gathered for celebrations
around the continent.
Players were there
with wood and wind instruments
and much brass to the left.
Drinks was flowing
vibes was kind of nice
I took my liquid cool y' know
leaving out the ice.

I stood firm in my position
defensive on the frontline.
Long in advance
I knew the bill
so I was looking forward
to a good showing
with vibrations
electro magnetics
radio activity.
Things going on from light
through to dark.

There was a singer on stage
who look like he love Isis
touching my hand, he offered me
the seat he had found.
Leading me to higher ground
the singer whispered softly
'I will reason with you and t'ing
after I done sing'.
So I settled
listening.

When all the explorers had gone
I stood on the stage
and saw the singer
standing by an exit.
He wanted me to search
for the fullness of his meaning
so I strained to hear.
Even in the electric light
I was leaning to the right
keen to know his story
and to find out for myself
if the plot was a study
written with love.

So I decided
not to leave the stage.
Finding comfort in remembering
the old folk saying
'those who don't deal with right
don't get bite they get eaten'.
Then Time said
'all hands off the deck
don't worry about
the face of the clock
everything must circle
to where I begin to start
again'.

Then light came streaming
through a window.
Standing still on stage
I saw the singer standing low
desperate to tell me something
before he was due to go.
Recalling the crowns of the explorers
and where we was sitting
our vision was marred.
Now we have rested
we can stand and can see
the party and the performance
are over.

When Time came
for another gathering
the explorers laughed
at that song about Columbus.
and the players sang a different tune.
The talk wasn't so conscious
the walk wasn't so high
and no one was paying
the respect due.

And so with the beat
of a distant drum
without a cross to bear,
we arise to walk
the eternal way again.
And so we strum and hum
the song of long gone ancients
whose souls abide here
waiting.

New explorers gather
celebrating around the continent,
so is the line of succession.
Pirate different to explorer
explorer different to we
I and I rise to a level
guided by our confession.
Understanding not fearing
Armageddon.

Hand Eye Coordination

Lightning Source UK Ltd.
Milton Keynes UK
UKIC01n2223050914
238174UK00007B/25

9 781477 237922